CONTENTS

Introduction

1 **Monday – How to Start**
   The clubs to buy and where to buy them. Other necessary
   equipment. The way to learn. The job of each club. Etiquette.
   Knowing the most important rules of the game.   1
2 **Tuesday – Understanding the Basics**
   Grip. Posture. Alignment. Ball position. Drills and exercises.   8
3 **Wednesday – The Golf Swing**
   The takeaway. Reaching the top of the backswing. The
   downswing, through impact and the follow-through. Using the
   different clubs.   22
4 **Thursday – The Short Game**
   100 yards and in. Around the greens. In the sand. Putting.   38
5 **Friday – More Advanced Golf**
   Fairway woods. Keeping the ball low. How to play the fade. How
   to play the draw. How to get backspin.   56
6 **Saturday – On the Course**
   Warming up. Course management. Dealing with problems.   66
7 **Sunday – Getting what you can out of the game**
   How to join a club. Getting a handicap. The different scoring
   systems. Playing competitions. Courses you can play.   81

Glossary   90

INTRODUCTION

Of course it is impossible to go from being a complete novice to an accomplished golfer in just seven days. This book does not pretend that one can. To do that in seven years would be quite an achievement!

What this book does aim to do is to offer a step-by-step guide to golf, taking you from buying your first clubs through to advanced golf and playing in various competitions.

It has been my aim to write as clearly and as concisely as possible but some golf instruction can be very difficult to follow and this could have a detrimental rather than a positive effect on your game. Ask a professional or a good player to check your progress to make sure you are on the right track.

This book is aimed first at the beginner, who should not be tempted to start just anywhere in the week but to work as the book is laid out – from Monday through to the weekend.

It may also be helpful to the seasoned low handicapper. In any sport, though perhaps more so in golf, one can lose one's way and with it one's confidence. To such, this book offers valuable revision. My game benefited from the actual writing of the book. Even the best players in the world are constantly checking their own games and making necessary changes. Each day the swing can feel a little different and adjustments must be made.

Above all, remember that golf is a unique game. Good players and beginners can compete with each other more happily than in any other sport; you can play on your own or with friends; you can take it very seriously or play just for fun – it has a lot to offer.

There may be times when frustration sets in and you feel like tossing your clubs away for good, but don't do that. Take up the challenge of the sport, figure out what you need to improve and work hard at it. Golf is a boom sport and for good reason.

Peter Oosterhuis

HOW TO START

. . . or more precisely, when to start. Remember you are never too young, never too old. There is no time like the present for a youngster to start swinging a club (albeit a shortened one) and, likewise, if you have reached retirement age don't consider that, as a recreation, golf has passed you by. What better way to spend your pension? And when you have started, like the most potent drug, golf is not something that can be easily discarded.

I am not going to pretend that golf is cheap. You can trek half way around the world on a tight budget but you cannot play golf on a shoestring. Club membership, equipment, lessons, golf holidays – they all mount up. Bear in mind that like any sport there can be no short cuts and you will find the rewards of golf immeasurable.

MONDAY

The clubs to buy and where to buy them

Until you are convinced that you and golf are set for some sort of relationship my advice is to hire a set from a local club professional, or better still, borrow from a friend. Then if you really find that you loathe the game you have not wasted any money.

Buying new clubs can be intimidating. There are simply so many of them: V-grooved, U-grooved, parabolic grooved; steel shafts, graphite shafts, boron shafts; wooden heads, metal heads, some cast in beryllium. Some come in different colours as the market becomes more fashion conscious. Which ones are for you, the beginner?

Ask a club pro for advice. That is part of his job. You don't have to be a member of the club to saunter into his shop and buy equipment. He may start you on a half set (one wooden club, 3-iron, 5-iron, 7-iron, 9-iron and putter) and see how you progress from there.

The key to buying clubs for the first time is to find a set that is suited to your physique, and rather than committing yourself to a whole set, choose from the lower priced open-ended range of clubs, those that can be bought individually and added to later.

To make sure that you are buying clubs that are right for you it is worth asking for custom-made clubs, made to your specific measurements, as you might visit a tailor and ask him to make you a suit. It takes time (about a fortnight) but it is well worth it. Most leading club manufacturers offer this service.

The alternative is to visit a high street sports shop or discount store where the prices may be a little lower, but the danger is to be blinded by science and sales talk from someone who, unlike the club pro, has no vested interest in your future. A salesman, quite possibly on some sort of incentive scheme, may be keen to shift stock which is not necessarily suitable to your physique. If a club pro shows concern equally for your golf game and your wallet you will be more inclined to ask him for lessons.

Other necessary equipment

When you have bought your clubs you will need something to put them in. Golf bags come in all sizes, and while it looks impressive to own a big bag sporting brand names and logos, they can be quite an effort to carry about.

If you start with a half set of clubs there is no point in having too big a bag, and as you acquire more clubs there are a variety of lightweight bags on the market. Imagine yourself on a golf holiday in a hot country. The last thing you want to do is lumber a heavy golf bag on and off the aeroplane and round the course. Buy light – buy cheap.

2

*Most pro shops stock a wide range of golf clubs
and accessories*

You will also need an umbrella (to keep your clubs dry as much as yourself) and some sturdy footwear, preferably with spikes. Whereas a golf glove is optional, a novice will need plenty of golf balls. New ones are expensive, so practice balls or rejects will do for starters until you have at least some control over where you are hitting them.

As for clothing, you can really wear what you like. As a rule private clubs prohibit denim jeans and T-shirts on the course, though municipal courses have no such sartorial rules. A pair of waterproofs to put into a compartment of your golf bag is also a good idea, Goretex being the best material since it allows the skin to breathe.

If you insist you can buy striped pullovers and shirts and checked trousers, but looking like a tournament golfer does not necessarily help you to play like one.

Remember that your dress should not restrict movement of the body, particularly the shoulders and hips, in any way. A far cry, indeed, from the pre-First World War days of the great Harry Vardon, who liked to play in a buttoned-up tweed jacket.

The way to learn

You will learn a great deal from the pages of this book, but you should still seek practical advice from your local golf pro. Golf has a habit of exposing flaws and weaknesses like no other sport. Lessons are vital for the beginner and recommended for the intermediate and advanced player. Imagine your golf swing as your health and the pro as your doctor. Never think that you are capable of curing a swing ailment yourself.

Bear in mind that even the very top players have their own favourite instructors whom they will see during their weeks off or in times of trouble. In fact they very often learn from each other, something which is evident if you watch the tournament pros on the practice-ground at an event.

Most golf clubs in Britain have a pro attached, some more expensive than others depending on their reputation. You don't need to be a member of the club to have a lesson.

Instruction schools are proving very popular. These are three or four day courses with groups of a similar standard under the guidance of some top coaches.

The job of each club

Before you start hitting a golf ball you must understand the function that each club serves. You are allowed 14 of them in your bag during a round of golf, but the beginner should not need that many.

The driver is the longest club in the bag and the most powerful. It is also the hardest to use and therefore not the first club with which to practise. Many players carry two more woods (they are easier to use for long shots from the rough), but should you find that you are a good iron player a 1-iron is a better addition to your armoury.

The angle of loft gradually gets greater as you work your way through the bag, so a 9-iron will not travel as far as a 5-iron but the trajectory will be higher.

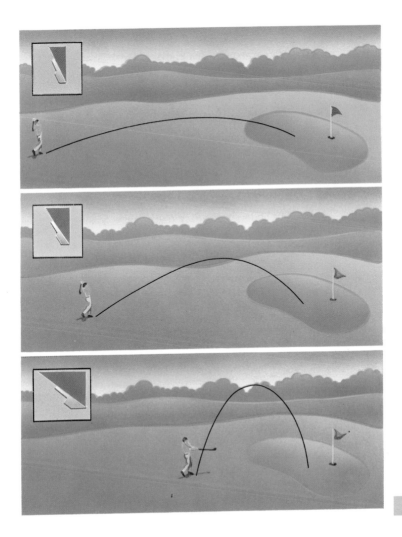

The hardest club to choose is probably the wedge as there are so many of them, all with different degrees of loft and different names – pitching wedge, lobber, 10-iron, etc. They are designed for the little delicate shots into and around the green.

The sand wedge is similar in appearance, but is used primarily in bunkers, the club's design being such that it passes neatly through the sand and under the ball.

The putter is possibly the single most important club in your bag. Good putting can save you so many strokes, so opt for a putter that not only gives you the best 'feel' but also looks 'right' to you.

These are only guide lines, aimed at the beginner. Equipment is a very personal part of the game, and you should play with whatever you feel is most comfortable.

Etiquette

Never overlook this vital facet of the game. It is as crucial as knowing how to play a bunker shot or a chip-and-run.

You may have the power of Greg Norman, the flair of Severiano Ballesteros and the determination of Jack Nicklaus, but if you have no clue about the etiquette of the game you are no golfer.

Etiquette is the game's code of behaviour. Treat fellow golfers on the course with the same amount of respect that you would wish to be shown yourself. Leave the course in at least the same condition as you found it. Rake bunkers, replace fairway divots and repair ball-mark blemishes on the greens.

Speed of play is imperative at all times. If people are being held up behind you call them through. Twoballs usually have right of way over three and fourballs, but each club has different 'house rules' and these should be strictly adhered to. It is this decorum that has helped establish for golf the untarnished image that it currently enjoys.

Knowing the most important rules of the game

Every sport has its rules – the 'what you can and what you can't do' on the field of play. Golf has more than most . . . many more! In fact to list each and every one now would fill this book.

The rules, laid down by the game's supreme governing bodies **The Royal and Ancient Golf Club of St. Andrews**, Scotland, and **The United States Golf Association**, are golf's highway code, but *The Rules of Golf* runs to over 100 pages, too much to learn by heart. Inevitably some are broken or bent during every round. Some are impractical, aimed

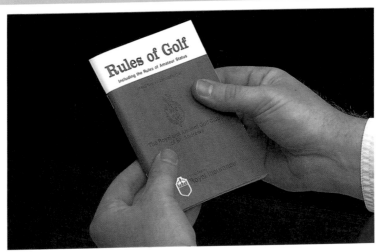

It's impossible to memorise all the rules of golf, but it's worth keeping this little book with you

primarily at the professional game, but the most important ones to commit to memory concern the penalties for lost balls and going out-of-bounds or into a hazard.

It is wise to carry a rule book in your bag for consultation, but as with any sport, the more you play, the more familiar you become with them all.

TUESDAY

UNDERSTANDING THE BASICS

There is an obvious temptation for beginners to think that the first lesson involves hitting the golf ball. Certainly that is what the game is all about, but succeeding in doing it successfully depends on how well the fundamentals of the swing have been understood.

Today we are going to concentrate on the set-up, incorporating the grip, posture, alignment and ball position. These vital factors are often overlooked. So much poor golf can be traced back to errors made in one of these four categories, which collectively form the backbone of a sound golf swing. If you start from a good address position it makes the execution of a good swing that much easier.

Grip

Many instruction books lead you to believe that there is only one proper way to grip the club, depending on the grip favoured by the author. Beginners tend to start by holding the club like a baseball bat which is not to be encouraged.

It can take some time for a grip to feel natural, but it is important to understand that a good, solid grip gives the clubhead a decent chance of returning squarely to the ball at impact. Remember that your hands are your only contact with the club.

There are two recommended grips and there are equally good cases for them both. These are the **overlapping** and the **interlocking**. The one for you is the one with which you feel most comfortable, although ladies and juniors, being in general less strong, may find the interlocking grip gives them greater strength and support on the club.

Overlapping

This grip is also known as the Vardon Grip, named after the great turn-of-the-century golfer, Harry Vardon, who was the first to grip the club in this manner. It is preferred by most tournament professionals today because it effectively marries the hands as one so that they behave as a unit.

Lay the club diagonally across your left palm so that the grip runs across the middle section of your index finger (vice versa for left-handers, obviously!). Make sure that you leave about one inch of the top of the club visible above your hands. Now close your palm over the club, with the thumb running down the grip, resting just right of centre. The 'V' between your thumb and index finger should point up to your right shoulder, with about two and a half knuckles of your left hand visible.

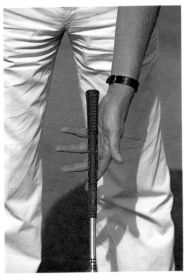

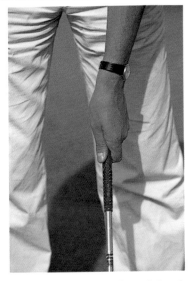

The grip of the club runs across the middle section of John's index finger. Also, about one inch protrudes above the hands

The thumb rests just right of centre on the grip and the 'V' between thumb and index finger points towards John's right shoulder

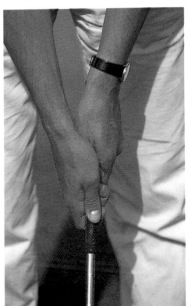

Then place the little finger of your right hand in the cleft between the first two fingers of your left hand and close the right hand over the thumb of the left. Your right thumb should rest fractionally to the left of the grip.

9

Interlocking

Again, take the club in the left hand, but this time place the index finger of your left hand between the little and third finger of the right hand. Now close the right hand over the thumb of the left.

Dinah illustrates the interlocking grip, recommended for weaker hands

Bad grips

The two most common faults one sees are when the hands 'move' on the club, resulting in either too weak or too strong a grip. When the hands are rotated to the right with all the knuckles showing on the left hand, this is called a strong grip and the tendency is to hook the ball, meaning that the clubhead will be closed at impact.

A weak grip is when the hands are rotated to the left, with the left hand too much under the shaft and the 'V' of the right hand pointing towards the left shoulder. Here the clubhead will be open at impact, resulting in a slice.

Another common fault among amateurs is the tendency to grip the club so tightly that it inhibits a fluid motion and discourages freedom of movement. Grip the club and then ask a friend to pull the club from your grasp. He should be able to do that without much effort. On the other hand do not hold the club so loosely that you lose control.

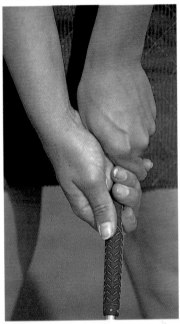

Above *Dinah's hands have rotated to the right – a strong grip.* **Below** *A weak grip results when the hands rotate to the left*

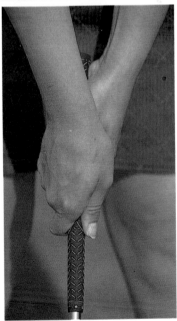

11

Posture

Now that the club has been gripped correctly, the next step is to stand properly and comfortably over the ball. Again, 'comfort' is a key word here; if you feel uncomfortable in your set-up there is less chance of a good swing.

For long shots stand with your feet about shoulder width apart. Both feet should be flat on the ground, with the weight distributed evenly between them, and on the balls and heels. Keep your back straight, bend forward a little from the hips and let your arms hang down in front of you. Your

A side-on view of the perfect posture

bottom should not fall into a sloppy position; try to convey the image of an athletic position, with springy legs and lightly flexed knees with the bulk of the tension in your thighs. You will naturally find that the shorter the club you have in your hand, the more you will lean over the ball.

The position of your head in the set-up is crucial. Again it should be comfortable, not with the chin tucked unnaturally into the chest, but held so that your shoulders can turn freely. Remember that the posture is designed to help, not hinder, your swing.

Alignment

It is remarkable how many players limit their chances of hitting the ball in the intended direction by making errors at this fundamental stage. If you are not lining up properly the ball is unlikely to go where you want it to.

For the longer shots your shoulders, hips and feet should be aligned parallel to the ball-to-target line. Imagine yourself on a railway-line with the ball and clubhead on the far rail and your feet on the near one.

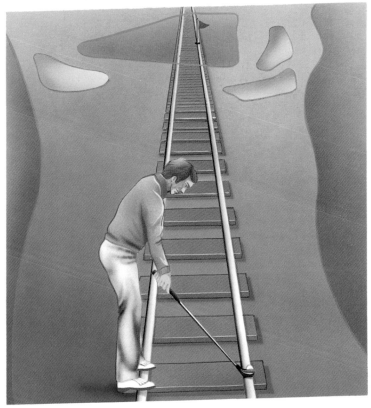

However, the closer you are to the green (in other words, if you have a 9-iron, wedge or sand-wedge in your hand) you can open your stance a little by pointing your feet fractionally left of target. Use the same swing and you will find that you are able to slice under the ball a little more, helping to stop the ball quickly on the green. This is quite technical, so perhaps is not something to be advised for the complete novice, but it is something to bear in mind as you progress.

There is also a tendency for beginners to have their feet too square (perpendicular to the target line) at address, which restricts the backswing coil and hinders a good follow-through. Imagine that you are standing in the middle of a giant clock and that your feet are hour hands. Your left foot should be pointing to the imaginary 11 on the clockface and your right foot halfway between the 12 and 1 on the clockface. The right foot should not be as open as the left because it is your right side that controls the hip turn in the backswing and the weight transferral must be onto the inside of your right foot for a good solid backswing.

Ball position

The positioning of the ball between the feet should vary according to which club you have in your hands, although some instructors advocate a constant ball position.

Remember that the longer the club the wider your stance should be, although even with the driver your stance should never be so wide that the insides of the feet are wider apart than the shoulders. Also the longer the club the further away you stand from the ball. Remember that your body should be about one hand's span from the butt of the club.

Another way of determining how far to stand from the ball is to let the top of the club rest against the left leg. Ideally it should fall about two or three inches above the knee. Any more than that and the stance is too cramped. If it falls on or below the knee you are reaching for the ball too much.

When it comes to positioning the ball in your stance, with the longest club in your bag (the driver) the ball should be opposite the inside of your left heel. For the long irons (2, 3 and 4), move the ball back (to the right) by about one inch and at the same time move the right foot closer to the left by the same amount – one inch.

For the medium irons (5, 6 and 7), move the ball a further one inch back towards the middle of your stance and likewise the right foot one inch closer to the left.

For the short irons (8, 9 and wedge), the ball is almost in the middle of the stance. Also the feet should be about three or four inches closer together than they were with the driver.

Drills and exercises

At the end of each day's tuition there are a number of drills and exercises that can be carried out, not only outside on the practice-ground, but also in your own home.

Grip

To help get the hands into the correct position, the neutral position as it is sometimes called, the 'clapping drill' is an excellent aid. Stand with your hands held down in front of your thighs. Start clapping, making sure that your fingers are pointed in the same direction, towards the ground. Then drop the right hand fractionally and take the grip as shown earlier. This is the position that your hands should adopt on the club, neither too far to the left or right.

For the correct right hand (lower hand) position on the club, imagine that you are shooting a pistol. The index finger is the trigger finger and has to be flexed accordingly. This is exactly the same position this finger has to adopt on the club.

Posture

There is one quick and very simple exercise to help you gain the correct posture over the ball. Stand up straight, then flex your knees, at the same time bending forward slightly from the waist. Then drop your hands down in front of you, like a gorilla!

Alignment

To check that your feet are aligned correctly place two clubs on the ground. One should be along the ball-to-target line and the other against your toes. The two clubs should be parallel to each other and will represent a square stance. If they are not parallel, your feet—and quite probably your hips and shoulders—are poorly aligned and the chances of hitting the ball in the intended direction are greatly reduced. Now place a third club on the ground to check the ball position.

John checks his alignment using parallel clubs

Keeping his clubhead in line with the divot, John knows he is aiming at the target

To help ensure that the clubface is pointing towards the target, as you take up your stance pick out a spot a few feet in front of you on the ball-to-target line. You should be able to keep that spot in vision as you prepare to play the shot.

Ball position

Now an excellent drill to help position the ball correctly in relation to your feet: adopt your normal set-up position and then place a tee peg in front of your toes. You can now walk away from the ball and return to it as many times as you like without fear of losing your good set-up position.

This exercise with two tee pegs helps you keep a good set-up position

THE GOLF SWING

At last! In this chapter you can finally hit the golf ball, and whether it travels anywhere in the intended direction depends entirely on how closely you follow the instructions.

However, golf is a very technical game so don't be surprised or unduly disappointed if at first your game is a bit awry. It can take many long, often frustrating hours on the practice-ground before it all comes together. But when it does, believe me, it's well worth it.

Whereas Tuesday's instruction provided the backbone to the golf swing, today's is the crux. If any one aspect of the swing falls out of kilter the likelihood of a good stroke is greatly reduced.

Although the full golf swing should be a free-flowing movement, it is easier at this stage to learn it step by step.

The takeaway

To non-golfers a takeaway is something you get from a Chinese restaurant. To the initiated it is the first few feet that the clubhead travels away from the ball at the start of the swing.

Take your normal address position as described in the last chapter. The secret of the takeaway is for the arms and wrists to be firm but relaxed, which does not mean tense and rigid because that restricts free-flowing movement, but then neither does it mean loose.

There is often a difference of opinion as to which hand governs the early part of the takeaway. In my opinion it should be the left, because if you start the takeaway with the right hand you tend to pick the club up too sharply, which makes it very difficult to get the club into the correct position at the top of the backswing.

Here Dinah has picked the club up too sharply, which will result in a chopping action on the downswing

You want to push, not pull, the clubhead away from the ball, so start the takeaway with the left hand as the dominant one, and see if you can keep the bottom of the club relatively close to the top of the grass for the first couple of feet. A good drill is to put a tee peg in the ground about two feet behind the ball and try to clip the top of it as you take the club back. Remember to keep the hands firm which will guarantee that the clubface does not open or close in this early stage of the backswing. In other words, do not cock the wrists. This will happen naturally later.

Reaching the top of the backswing

As I have already said, the swing should be one rhythmic motion, but should a fault creep in it will be easier to spot by breaking the swing down into a number of stages.

As the club continues its path to the top of the backswing the most important thing to remember, which sadly many handicap golfers do not, is that the body should not make any unnecessary movements. If it does, the chance of making a good solid contact with the ball is lessened. The body should **rotate**, not lurch or sway, with the head remaining in the same position over the ball.

The best drill to help you rotate rather than sway is to hold the butt of a club into your navel, as these three pictures illustrate

A good exercise is to stand straight up with the butt of a golf club in your navel, keeping the club in that position as you turn a full 90 degrees to the right, remembering to keep your head facing forward. Now turn back, past the point level with your head and through to 90 degrees to the left, allowing your head to follow.

Now adopt the orthodox address position and try to repeat this exact motion. This is the rotation effect that is the essence of a good backswing. It helps the trunk to turn and more importantly, it helps the shoulders to turn, not tilt, so that by the time you have reached the top of the backswing the shoulders have rotated to the extent that the top of the back is facing directly at the target.

As the backswing reaches the top you should transfer the bulk of your weight to the inside of the right foot, but ensure at the same time that both knees remain flexed as they were at address. The left knee should have turned in, slightly towards the right.

You should now have some idea how the body works in the backswing, but the next question is – how do the arms work? Well, as long as they work as a unit with the body turn, you do not really have to worry about them. At address the right elbow should be loosely tucked into the right side of the chest, and here it should stay throughout the backswing. The left arm should be relatively straight and only when the arms are parallel with the ground should the wrists begin to cock.

A handkerchief under the arm helps create a compact turn, the secret being to ensure that it remains in place throughout the swing

Another good drill is to keep a handkerchief tucked under the right arm. As you carry out the backswing, the handkerchief should remain in place, helping to create a more compact turn. If it does not the probability is that you are swinging on too upright a plane.

Now, what about the hands? There can be a danger of trying to follow instructions too exactly and letting technicalities get in the way of a rhythmic swing. It would be unwise to try and **place** your hands in the correct positions during the backswing, but there is one point to bear in mind.

When you reach the top of the backswing, ask a friend to check that the back of your left hand is square to the clubface. This is generally regarded as the neutral position, enabling you to hit the ball hard, safe in the knowledge that the clubface is in the ideal position to hit the ball dead straight.

Another good pointer to help get the perfect right hand position at the top of the backswing is to imagine that you are carrying a drinks tray in the way that a waiter does.

A popular topic for debate is how long the backswing should be. Ideally the club should reach horizontal, something which comes with practice, but you will see many top professionals either fall fractionally short of the horizontal, or, more rarely, exceed it. Either way, it is no great sin, but the secret is to have a length of swing that you can control.

This is the ideal position at the top of the backswing. Notice that from behind the clubhead is pointing directly at the target.

The downswing, through impact and the follow-through

The ideal swingpath for the club on the downswing and through impact is 'in-to-out' or hitting from the inside, as opposed to 'out-to-in'. This automatically helps to **draw** the ball (right to left), which gives you further distance than a **fade** (left to right).

Left Dinah is hitting from the inside, as her right elbow is still close to the right side of the body. Below Hitting too much with the right shoulder causes this 'out-to-in' swingpath

The first motion on the downswing is in the shoulders which pull the hands and arms down in the same way that a bellringer pulls on a bell-rope. This will help the club start its downward path on the correct plane, increasing the likelihood of an in-to-out hit.

There is a great tendency to 'come over the top' of the ball, a common fault caused by the right shoulder starting the downward movement. This results in a severe pull or slice or, most destructive of the lot, a shank. Many people believe that to achieve a powerful hit one must hit hard from the shoulders. That is wrong. It is the arms and ultimately the hands that generate the clubhead speed that leads to maximum distance. Imagine the downward path being the same as that for the backswing, with the right elbow still tucked loosely into the chest as it was at address, As you reach about halfway down, the weight should shift onto the left side and the wrists begin to uncock naturally.

Another common fault at this stage is that, as the weight shifts onto the left side, so the head moves left as well. That only leads to disaster, and is known as 'getting ahead of the ball', the most common result being a push to the right. Keep the head in exactly the position it was at address, concentrating on looking at the back of the ball (using the manufacturers name as a target is always a good tip on the tee). The head should remain in this position until just after impact, when it is important to allow it to come up with the arms so as not to restrict the follow-through, and also so that you can see where the ball goes!

There is a myth that the head should stay stock still throughout the golf swing, an anomaly which can lead to being too rigid. What it really means is that you should keep your eye on the ball, something which is nigh impossible if you jerk the head around.

The follow-through is different from the rest of the swing in so far as it does not require specific positioning of the body. A good follow-through is the result of a good downswing, but there are a few pointers in the follow-through to help you gauge whether the downswing has been satisfactory.

This is how your follow-through ought to look. The top of the right shoulder is under the chin, the club is over the left shoulder, the spine is straight and most crucial of all, the weight is on the left foot. How often I see players rocking back onto their right foot after they have struck the ball. The result of this is a drastic loss of power at impact, and hence loss of distance. In fact, when you have finished your follow-through, try and lift the right foot off the ground. If you can hold this position for a while it proves that you have a comfortable, well-balanced follow-through.

Another common fault is an abbreviated follow-through, which is a clear giveaway that there has not been enough acceleration at impact, the force of which should carry you into a high finish. Remember I was saying that at the top of the backswing, the point between your shoulders should be pointing at the target. Well, at the end of the follow-through your navel should be pointing at the target. This shows how much the golf swing demands a full shoulder turn, both before impact and after.

Using the different clubs

Having briefly learned the difference between each club in the first chapter, it is now time to learn how to use each club. There should really be no great difference in the way you swing a wooden club and the way you swing a long or short iron. It is merely the angle of attack that alters: because a wooden club is longer than a 9-iron or wedge, the distance you stand from the ball increases and the arc is bigger and wider.

Wooden clubs

One uses a wooden club for distance, whether it's a driver from the tee or a 3-wood from the fairway, so the angle of attack on the ball should maximise that. That means a sweeping motion into the ball, driving it forward with a minimum of backspin.

There is a tendency to try and hit the ball too hard with the driver. Its straight face already guarantees extra distance, so the secret is to swing with control. It is better for the ball to travel 220 yards down the fairway than 250 yards in the thick rough.

Long and medium irons

For handicap golfers, the long irons are regarded as the hardest clubs in the bag to use, while the mid-irons seem to be the easiest. This is because long irons have straighter faces and less margin for error.

With, say, a 3-iron, the angle of attack is slightly steeper than it would be for a driver, but you should not try and make a conscious effort to achieve this. It should occur naturally as a result of standing fractionally closer to the ball, and with the stance a little narrower.

Short irons

People mistakenly think that the shorter the club, the easier the shot. How wrong can they be. These clubs are instruments of accuracy, and though it may be true that a slice with a wedge will not go so far off line as a slice with a driver, the majority of short iron shots are played to the flag, so that argument is small consolation.

Again, one stands closer to the ball, with a narrower and more open stance. This will automatically provide a steeper angle of attack on the ball, helping impart backspin and ensuring greater height on the shot.

THE SHORT GAME

Undeniably this is the most important facet of the game – the scoring zone, as many people like to call it. You can have an indifferent long game, but if you have a recuperative short game then your scores will emerge looking respectable.

Compare these two games: Player A hits a booming drive, then hits the green before three putting. Player B hits a very weak drive and has to play a recovery shot into the fairway. He then pitches to five feet and single putts. Who wins the hole? Player B, and solely on the strength of his short game.

A player with a good short game is one with good 'feel'. He can envisage the type of shot required for the best result, maybe a high floater over a hazard, or a chip-and-run with a straight faced club. But it takes a great deal of practice to get a good short game. There is a temptation on the practice-ground to thrash balls endlessly into the distance with your big guns, but he who spends the majority of his time working on his short game will probably emerge as the player shooting the lower scores.

Then there's putting. The inability to hole a putt at a crucial time has been the ruination of many a great championship golfer over the years. It may look simple, but it is not. There is a thin line between a holed putt and one that lips out.

This may very well be the most important day's instruction of the week.

100 yards and in

The pitch shot

With a pitch the ball spends more time in the air than on the ground, the idea being to send the ball up on a fairly high trajectory so that it will land softly, and stop on the green as quickly as possible.

The hardest thing about this shot is that you must be able to hit the ball various distances; at one hole you may be 30 yards from the green, at the next twice that distance, and in both circumstances you may want to use a sand wedge. There are no short cuts, only practice can build up 'feel'. Hitting a whole bag of balls to imaginary flags at various distances can help develop this 'feel'.

To play the shot, take up a narrow, open stance, with the clubface aimed at the hole. The weight should be predominantly on the left foot, where it should remain throughout the swing.

John illustrates the ideal stance for the pitch shot, feet pointing left of target, clubface directly at it

This is the ideal backswing for a pitch shot, short and compact, with the club picked up on a steeper plane than usual

The swing for this shot is mainly with the hands and arms, keeping both firm through impact. Try to avoid any exaggerated body movement. Pick the club up a little more steeply than usual, bringing it down on an identical plane. Remember not to overswing. The secret is to keep the swing short and compact.

The chip-and-run

In contrast, with this shot the ball will spend only a short time in the air before it runs along the ground to the hole, so obviously it cannot be played if hazards are between the ball and the green.

Again you need to have a narrow, open stance with the weight on the front foot but the ball in the middle of your stance. You may opt for a straighter faced club than the wedge, but generally it is a case of how you visualise the shot and how far you are from the green.

Unlike the pitch, the club should be taken back on an inside path and no more than a half swing should be necessary. As with the full swing, remember not to 'get ahead' of the ball at impact; in other words, minimise upper body movement on the downswing, keeping the head behind the ball at impact.

The chip-and-run is an ideal shot to play in parched conditions, when the greens are very firm and there is little benefit in hitting a high pitch which is unlikely to stop quickly on the greens. It is worth practising this shot as much as possible. It is a very useful addition to one's armoury, and you would be surprised how many times an imperfectly struck shot gets satisfactory results.

Around the greens

Shots that are played from just off the green, or even on the fringe of it, are really an extension of putting, so in the same way as you would read the line and break on a putt, so too when chipping from this distance.

There is no rule as to which club you should use. It is a question of going with the one with which you feel most comfortable. If that is an 8-iron, bear in mind that the ball will travel with less elevation than if you used a 9-iron or wedge. If you have to play to an elevated green there may be no option but to play the shot with a sand wedge for extra loft, so it is worth practising these dainty little shots with the 8-iron through to the sand wedge.

You need to pre-plan the shot. First, pick out a point on the green where you think the ball should land, taking into account borrow and the green's firmness. This should be your preliminary target. Forget about the hole itself.

For tighter control, grip down the club. Take up an open stance, this time with the feet almost together and with the ball in line with the right heel. The hands should be slightly ahead of the ball.

This is very much a hands and arms swing. As with the chip-and-run, take the club back on the inside and be sure not to 'quit' on the ball; do not decelerate at impact, which usually leads to fluffing the shot. Be confident, keep the swing short and compact with the hands firm at impact.

However, there is one thing to bear in mind: if you are just off the green, no more than a few feet from the fringe without any rough interfering, putt the ball. A bad putt is often equal to a good pitch, as any instructor will tell you.

In the sand

Often an area of panic. Time and again people tell themselves that they cannot play a good bunker shot, merely because they see a bunker as a frightening hazard. There is a secret to playing out of bunkers, and it is not a difficult one to grasp.

In a greenside bunker use a sand wedge. They generally have greater bounce (angle on the sole), allowing the clubhead to glide smoothly through the sand. They also have the greatest degree of loft, throwing the ball into the air quickly so that it will land 'softly' on the greens.

The basic bunker shot

As with the pitch shot, take an open stance in the bunker, working the feet into the sand so that they feel stable. Then open the clubface a little, making sure that it still points in the direction that you want the ball to fly. The more open the clubface, the more elevation the ball will get, though obviously it will travel a shorter distance. Also choke down slightly on the grip of the club, but be careful not to ground the club in the sand. That incurs a one shot penalty.

Here Dinah has a comfortable open stance and her clubface is not touching the sand behind the ball

From behind, you can see that Dinah is taking the club back outside the target line, along the line of her feet

The idea of adopting this stance is that you will want to swing the club along the line of the feet, which, as well as the shoulders and hips, are pointing left of the target. As long as the clubface is positioned correctly you should not need to worry about the flightpath of the ball. In other words the club should be taken back outside the target line, encouraging an out-to-in swingpath, the opposite to that required for a full shot from the tee or fairway.

It must be remembered that the clubface should slide **under** the ball. No direct impact with the ball is made; instead it is the sand which throws the ball out of the bunker, so concentrate on hitting about one inch behind the ball. This shot is primarily a hands and arms motion, so try and keep the lower body stable.

Pick out the spot where the clubhead will enter the sand. A helpful tip is to imagine that the ball is lying on a thin strip of material in the bunker and that your aim is to scoop the material, with the ball on it, out and onto the green.

A common fault is to decelerate at impact, which usually results in leaving the ball in the bunker. Be sure to hit confidently through the ball.

Perhaps the main reason why bunker shots strike such fear into the minds of handicap golfers is that they never practise them. Every time you set foot on the practice-ground take time to hit some bunker shots to flags at various distances. Experiment with clubface angles and amounts of power for the different length shots you may face on the course.

Dinah and John practise hitting bunker shots of varying distances

The long bunker shot

Whereas the standard bunker shot is relatively simple, this one is anything but, although part of the problem may be psychological.

If you are playing from a fairway bunker and still feel that reaching the green is a realistic possibility, it can be worthwhile using an extra club. But beware of being too ambitious. You do not want to catch the lip of the bunker in front of you, so first make sure that you have enough elevation to escape, even if it means just playing down the fairway.

For all long bunker shots the stance should not be as open as it is for the basic sand shot, and the feet should be as far apart as for a fairway shot of the same distance.

The swing should resemble more closely the orthodox long iron or wood shot; in other words a shallower plane, taking the club back in a more sweeping motion. On the downswing, try to hit the ball first, then the sand. Sand first and then ball would make a slightly 'fat' impact, and the ball will fall way short of its destination. You want the ball to fly forwards on a lower and more powerful trajectory.

A point to remember: it is easier to play long bunker shots with irons than woods. A wood tends to bounce off the sand, causing an imperfect strike.

Putting

Whole books have been written on putting alone, indicating that it is unquestionably the most important single facet of the game. Its importance cannot be over-emphasised. For every hour spent on the practice-ground, two should be spent on the putting green. *You drive for show and putt for dough* is the most often quoted adage in golf.

There is no hard and fast rule about how to putt. It is all a case of personal taste and comfort. If it goes in the hole then it works. Take the great Gary Player for example. Despite his diminutive frame he stoops over the ball, takes the putter back with a very wristy action, and stabs at the ball. Probably not recommended for novices, but it worked for him.

American Ray Floyd stands very upright and very open to the hole. Bernhard Langer almost invented the 'cack-handed' method, with his left hand below right, and despite his weaknesses, statistics show that he has a very good record on the greens.

Ray Floyd favours an upright open stance

The unusual 'cack-handed' method of Bernhard Langer

Unlike any other shot in golf, putting demands a different grip. There is the ten-finger grip, where all ten fingers are gripping the club, which may suit some, but I prefer the reverse overlap. The index finger of the left hand should either fall into the cleft between the last two fingers of

There's little difference between these two solid putting grips, but on the right, John's left index finger runs almost all the way down the fingers of his right hand

the right hand, or it should fall across all the fingers of the right hand. This helps to keep the left hand firm through the stroke, keeping the putter head on target.

The first important step is to get the correct ball position. It is really very simple if you remember this drill: take your stance and hold a ball to the bridge of your nose, then let it drop to the ground. Mark where it lands and move it one ball's width closer to you. This should be where you stand in relation to the ball; in other words with it directly below your eyes.

Your stance should be square to the hole. This helps to align the shoulders properly. Some teachers prefer their stance to be a little open, but there has to be compensation for that in the stroke. Keeping everything square helps to consistently deliver the putter-face squarely at impact.

The role of the hands and arms when putting is crucial. The hands should be quite close to the body. If they are too far away it is difficult to keep a well-grooved, repeating stroke. Keep the elbows bent and tucked into the body.

When gripping the club, the hands should be neutral; in other words one particular hand should not be the dominant one on the club. Too strong a right hand may pull the ball. Too strong a left hand encourages a push.

THURSDAY

When you begin the backswing to the putt you do not want to make too wristy a stroke, despite Gary Player's success. Keep the hands firm and, as before, imagine the putter as an extension of the left arm. The danger here is of turning the shoulders. They should stay on the same plane throughout the stroke. As the putter head goes back the left shoulder should drop. As you follow through the right one drops. It is like a clock pendulum; the clock face is your head, unable to move as the pendulum swings back and forth.

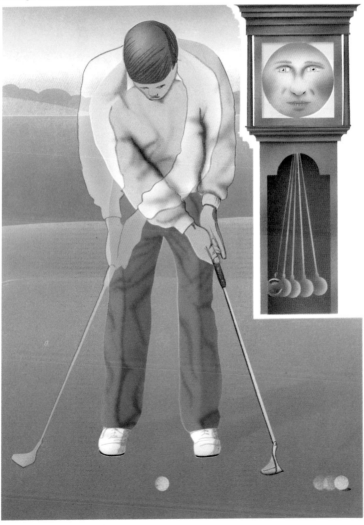

Dinah practises her putting stroke with the use of tee pegs

The putter head passes between the tee pegs after impact

This drill should help with the backswing: place some tee pegs in the ground, a little wider apart than the length of the putter head. As you take the putter back from the ball it must pass between the tee pegs, as it must through impact. This helps to develop a good line in the takeaway.

The great sin on hitting the ball is to decelerate at impact, particularly on short putts. Keep an even pace throughout the stroke, again like the clock pendulum.

This is the basic putting stroke, but there is a strategy to putting which can help your scores.

After impact the follow-through is crucial to a successful putt. First, the putter should follow through towards the hole, and second, concentrate on making the follow-through the same length as your backswing.

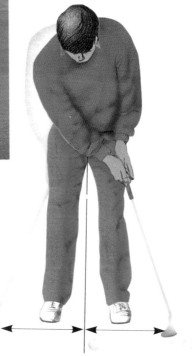

The par of a hole permits two putts and sometimes, if you are a great distance from the hole, you should concentrate on trying to use them both. Draw an imaginary five-foot circle around the hole and try to putt the ball into the circle. Your next putt will be a very 'makeable' one. It is very good practice for gauging the right distance.

On short putts, the ones that you would expect to make, say, eight times out of ten, you are faced with two options. You may either prefer to hit the ball firmly at the hole disregarding any slope, or alternatively, roll it gently taking the slope into account and planning for it to die into the cup. Either way is satisfactory, but what is not satisfactory is second-guessing, when you plan the stroke but change your mind just before impact. Choose a method and stick to it or the result will be fatal. Always remember another golfing adage: 'never up, never in'. In other words, if a ball doesn't drop, at least give it a chance of doing so.

That said, bear this in mind: when one is left with a short putt, putting uphill is much simpler than downhill. There is no need to fear striking the ball confidently into the heart of the hole. Take this into account before taking your first putt or chipping from off the green.

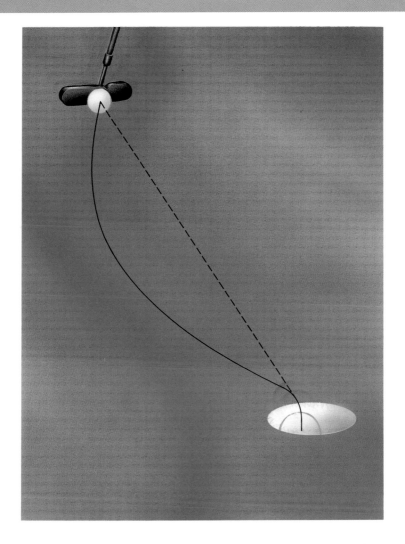

Reading the break or **borrow** on a green comes with experience. Make it easier for yourself by taking note of how the ball rolls on the green after your approach shot. Have a quick look at the line of the putt from behind the ball, but there is no need to take as much time as the tournament professionals do. Then, as you stand over the ball lining up the putter head, imagine how you think the ball is going to roll towards the hole and how much pace you need to apply. Too many handicap golfers just go up to the ball and hit and hope for the best without really giving much thought to the stroke.

MORE ADVANCED GOLF

So far you have learnt the bare essentials. If you have mastered them you can score well on the golf course, but sometimes circumstances demand that the ball must follow a specific path, or you need to stop the ball quickly on the green. To reach your full potential it is important that you learn how to manufacture a shot, and that you get the very most from the clubs you have in your bag.

Fairway woods

Long irons are still considered easier to use on the fairway than wooden clubs, but if it's distance you are after, rather than safety, you need to be proficient with woods from all positions on the course.

Nowadays most players carry a driver and a 3-wood in their bag; handicap golfers may also carry a 4- or a 5-wood, while some professionals favour a 1-iron. It is not impossible to hit a driver from the fairway, but it is really difficult. A well struck 3-wood shot should be enough in most circumstances.

To hit a wood from the fairway the ball should be lying cleanly. If it's lying down a little take an iron, because you can then use a steeper swing arc. The extra length of a wooden club means that you must use a wider arc on the swing.

Your stance for the shot should be very similar to the drive off the tee – a square stance and set-up to the ball, the feet and shoulders parallel to the target. Widen your stance a little more than for an iron shot, allowing yourself a more solid base for a powerful swing.

Even without the ball on a tee peg you need the shallowest descent into the ball, so the widest arc possible is required. Do not start picking the club up on the backswing until you really have to. In other words, keep a good left arm extension until your trunk has to rotate. Allow yourself a very full shoulder turn before starting the downswing. Similarly, after impact, have a full follow-through, this time keeping your right arm extended for as long as possible.

These days club manufacturers are making 6- and 7-woods, particularly favoured among lady golfers. But remember, the elevation on a 5-wood is greater than it is on a 2-iron, so if the wind is strong consider well before you select a lofted fairway wood.

Keeping the ball low

The ability to keep the ball low while still hitting it a decent distance is particularly useful when the wind is strong.

Whenever I played in the Open Championship on links courses I was grateful for the ability to hit low shots under the wind. Imagine a strong headwind. If you hit a shot with a normal elevation, the ball will reach a certain height and then be almost blown backwards.

Another time a low shot is not only useful but essential is when one needs to hit a shot under an overhanging branch.

Executing a low punch is not really difficult. It is a matter of having confidence in the stroke.

If the distance to the green usually requires, say, an 8-iron, then take a 6-iron or even a 5-iron. Grip a little lower than usual on the club, position the ball a little further back than halfway between the feet, keeping the hands ahead of the ball. Your stance should be slightly open, as it would be for a wedge shot.

The backswing should be on a steep plane, stopping well short of the horizontal – no more than a three-quarter swing – before attacking the ball with the hands and arms. Try and keep the body as still as possible during the entire swing. It is a hands and arms motion. There is a big temptation to drive the body and head forward at impact. Keep them still, in the same position they were at address.

For this low punch shot, John grips down the shaft and uses only a three-quarter swing, keeping his head still throughout

To punch the ball you must hit the ball first, turf second, then try and keep the follow-through limited to about halfway.

How to play the fade

An average golfer is happy just to hit the ball straight, but there are times when one needs to bend the ball in a certain direction – trees may be in the way, for example, or alternatively, although no hazard interferes with the route to the green, a certain shape of shot may still be advisable; imagine a pin cut on the right hand side of the green with a perilous bunker just off the right side, waiting to snatch a shot that has been too ambitious and narrowly failed. The ideal shot here is a fade, making full use of the wide expanse of green, but with the shape of the shot still carrying the ball towards the flag.

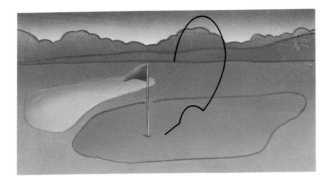

Most tournament professionals play with a fade when they need a shot that can be controlled. The ball will land softer, so it is particularly useful in hard conditions.

No dramatic swing or set-up changes are necessary. If the clubface is turned fractionally open the ball will obviously fly left to right.

What you are imparting is cutspin, so take at least one longer club than you would normally. Make sure that the clubface is pointing at the target, but align the feet and shoulders slightly open, parallel with the line that you want the ball to start its flight.

61

The ball should be positioned forward in the stance. Concentrate on having the club under good control with the left hand.

The backswing should be the same as usual. At the top the club should be pointing slightly to the left of the intended target, and the downswing made along the line of the feet and shoulders. Through impact keep a relaxed right hand, and do not let the right hand roll over the left. You want the left hand to be just ahead of the right at impact, or, in other words, in control, not allowing the right hand to close the clubface.

The bigger you want the fade to be, the more open the clubface should be. You may also need a more out-to-in swing; in other words picking the club up a little sharper, and slightly cutting across the ball at impact. Concentrate on the follow-through ending up just to the left of the original flight line.

How to play the draw

Knowing how to play the draw is useful for three main reasons. First, you may need to bend the ball right to left around some trees. Second, the pin might be tucked into the left hand side of the green, and a draw will guard against flirting with any danger that may be just off the left side of the green. And third, a draw guarantees extra distance as the shot flies lower and has less backspin. But beware, it is not such an easy ball to control upon landing, so in dry and hard conditions it is not advisable, and it can be a disadvantage on a narrow course.

As with the fade, the feet and shoulders should be aligned in the direction that you want the ball to start its flight, not where you want it to finish. Put the ball slightly behind centre in the stance.

The backswing should follow the line of the feet and shoulders, so that at the top of the backswing the club is pointing slightly to the right of its intended destination.

On the downswing, follow the line of the feet and shoulders, but through impact the right hand *should* roll over the left. This has the effect of closing the clubface at impact, causing the ball to bend right to left. You will also notice that at impact the right elbow is much closer to the chest than it would be for the fade.

But do remember that a draw produces more roll, so club down.

How to get backspin

You will find yourself in certain positions on the course when backspin is vital if you're to leave yourself a realistic opportunity of one-putting. Imagine having to hit a pitch over a hazard with little green to work onto. The ball may only bounce twice at the most before it must stop abruptly.

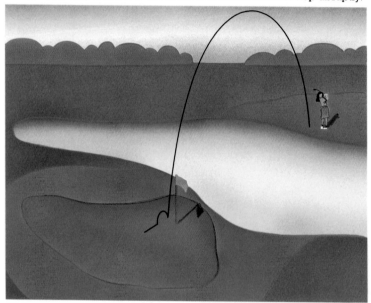

One important key to getting backspin does not require shotmaking at all – if the grooves on the club are not clean it will not make a clean impact on the ball. Clean grooves 'grip' the ball, helping it to stop quickly on landing. To remove dirt from the grooves use a golf towel or the end of a tee peg.

It is easier to get backspin on the ball with a shorter club than with a long one. This is because one uses a much steeper swing arc with the shorter irons. So remember to open your stance for the shorter irons, encouraging a steeper descent on the ball, which increases the chance of making contact first with the ball, then with the turf, rather than vice versa. This has the same effect as striking a billiard ball near the bottom with the tip of the cue. It neutralises forward spin.

ON THE COURSE

Up till now you have had instruction on how to play shots – putts, bunker shots, drives, chips with backspin and so on. But so far all of this has been practice-ground tuition; when you finally get out on the course you run into situations that are either difficult to practise or often neglected.

You will encounter problems germane only to a golf hole. Instead of cursing your bad luck, be ready to recover from them without damaging your score.

Preparation is important. Golf is a tough enough game as it is without making it harder. Allow yourself every chance of playing your best golf every time you tee up. Remember that only about 80 per cent of golf is shotmaking.

Warming up

Frequently a handicap golfer will walk straight from the club house to the first tee, pull out his driver, and after a couple of cursory practice swings hit a poor shot. Then he gets cross that the ball hasn't sailed 250 yards straight down the middle of the fairway. Some chance!

Not only does this lack of preparation usually damage a score, but more importantly it can damage a body as well, particularly the lower back.

In a golf swing some unnatural positions are demanded, and the body should always be prepared for this. A good warm-up ensures longevity.

Try to allow yourself at least 20 minutes on the practice-ground. This grooves your swing and also loosens the muscles. If the practice-ground is some distance from the first tee or you are beginning your round at the 10th, there are a number of little warm-up drills to loosen you up.

Make some practice swings with two or even three clubs in your hand. Swing casually. The extra weight will loosen the muscles.

Another favourite is to put a club behind your back and turn your torso as you simulate the golf swing. Try not to sway. This gets your body moving as it should even before you hit your first shot.

Do not forget to hit a few putts on the putting-green before starting. This will not warm up any muscles in your body as such, but it will give you a feel of how fast the greens are playing, and the putting-green is often the only yardstick available to you. Insure against any dangers of frittering away needless strokes.

Opposite above *Swinging with more than one club*
Opposite below *Turn your torso with clubs behind your back*

Course management

This is another area of the game where good preparation can save shots. All it needs is a little common sense and forward planning. Think your way around the course with every shot you take. For example, on the first tee ask yourself what shot you think will bring you the greatest reward, bearing in mind your limitations. Then ask yourself that question before every shot.

If you are stuck behind a tree and only a big fade would get you anywhere near the green, but you know you have never hit a decent fade intentionally in your life, don't attempt the shot. Knock the ball into the heart of the fairway and see if you can recover the stroke from there, rather than run the high risk of a disaster with a rash stroke.

Course management also consists of knowing roughly how far you are capable of hitting the ball with each club.

When hitting into a green observe the pin position. You may be, say, 150 yards from the centre of the green, a perfect distance for a 7-iron, but if the pin is at the back of the green, 10 feet past centre, you might need a 6-iron.

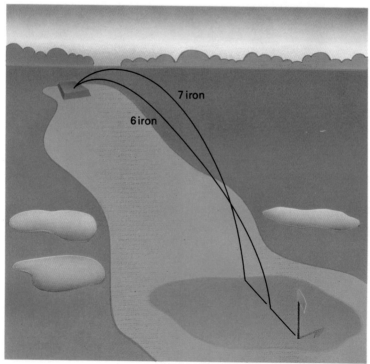

When teeing off consider which way the fairway slopes. If it's right to left you will want to try and fade the shot into the fairway to counteract the slope. A left to right slope demands a draw.

Dealing with problems

Different lies

One of the things the practice-ground does not allow for is the variation of lies you may encounter in a round of golf. Practice-grounds tend to be flat, but you cannot expect to go a whole 18 holes with your ball lying cleanly in the fairway every time. Depending on your lie you may need to alter your stance, posture, ball position or swing, and possibly all at the same time.

Ball below feet When the ball is below the level of your feet you need to change your posture, bending a little more from the waist, and to change the ball position, standing a little closer. Both these changes are obvious because of the extra distance you have to reach for the ball.

Make sure you keep the weight on your heels. You don't want to lose balance just before impact.

When the ball lies below the level of your feet you will find that it has a natural tendency to fade, a result of the swing being more upright than normal, so it is worth aiming a little left of the target and perhaps taking one extra club.

Dinah has the weight on her heels and she's bending more than usual from the waist

The natural lie of the ball encourages a more upright swing than usual

Ball above feet I could save time and space by saying that to play this shot well you have to do almost the exact opposite of when the ball is below your feet. Stand further away from the ball with the weight to the front of the feet. The swing will have to be on a flatter plane, forcing a more in-to-out arc. As a result the ball will draw, so take a club less and aim a little right of the target.

Left *Here, Dinah's weight is more on the front of her feet.* Below *A wider swing arc is needed for this stance*

Uphill lie   Another example of an inconsistent lie is when you discover the ball lying on an uphill slope.

The first thing to remember is that the ball will fly higher, but not so far, so take an extra club. Then, when you take your stance, bend the left knee a little to level up the line of your waist and shoulders as much as possible. Inevitably your weight will fall back onto the right foot, but try

and keep it on the inside of the foot, so that when you make your turn you don't commit the cardinal sin – swaying and not turning.

The lack of weight transfer to the left side during the shot means the ball will draw.

Downhill lie   The downhill slope means that the ball will fly lower and as a result further, so take a club less. This time bend the right knee a little to bring together the line of your waist and shoulders, and in the takeaway pick the club up a little more sharply than you would otherwise, to avoid catching it on the ground behind the ball. Your weight will tend to fall onto the front foot, but even so, a weight shift onto the right foot during the backswing and then onto the left foot just before impact is by no means impossible. With this shot the ball will have a tendency to fade.

SATURDAY

Playing from a divot

These shots can be practised on the practice-ground, but no-one ever has the foresight to do so.

One of the most frustrating things that can happen is to hit a perfect drive and have the ball roll into a divot, all because some inconsiderate person in a group ahead has not bothered to obey one of the most important points of etiquette in golf – that divots must be replaced.

To play this shot successfully set up normally. To force the ball out of the divot you need an upright swing so that you hit the back of the ball with a descending blow. This will send the ball forward on a low trajectory, and it will land with more roll.

Playing from the rough

There is seldom rough on practice-grounds, so that the only time you ever get a chance to play from it is out on the course itself. Thick rough is obviously a curse; you may lose your ball for one thing. But light rough is not difficult to play from as long as you hit through the ball solidly and confidently and allow for the occasional flyer – when rough gets between the ball and clubface at impact, causing the ball to shoot off the clubface and a little further than intended. This is all very well when you are playing down the fairway, but not such a laugh when playing an approach into the green.

A good point to remember is that a lofted wooden club glides through rough better than a long iron; grass can often become tangled around the clubface of an iron, turning it slightly and forcing the ball off-line.

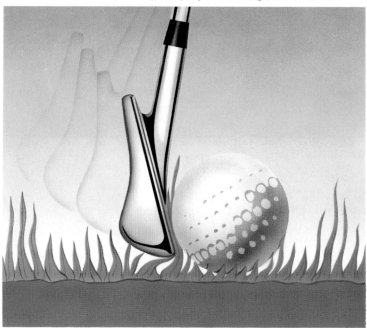

Thick rough is a different matter altogether. It is not uncommon on some courses to have to play a shot from such deep rough that it appears never to have been cut!

The first secret is not to be too ambitious. Accept the fact that you may not reach the green. Take a club that guarantees an escape from the rough – usually a lofted one – rather than being too greedy and running the risk of only moving the ball a few feet.

Set up normally, with the ball opposite the right heel. Take a firm grip on the club and pick it up sharply, allowing a sharp descent into the ball. Then just hit it hard with a full follow-through. You want to give yourself every chance of moving it the maximum distance.

A good tip to bear in mind if the grass is covering the ball is not to ground the club; you may inadvertently move the ball at address, incurring a penalty shot. It will also help you get a smooth takeaway.

Escaping from serious trouble

In theory a really good golfer should not get into serious trouble. In reality, he does . . . quite often, and it is how he recovers from it that determines how good his final score is.

What constitutes serious trouble? Well, having to play a bunker shot with one foot in and one foot out of the hazard, or playing out of an inch or two of water when the ball has rolled into a water hazard, or playing with your back to the target after your ball has come to rest against a tree or a wall, or playing a shot on your knees or with a left-handed swing.

Let us start with the awkward bunker shot. The first mistake when the ball is close to the back lip is to try and keep both feet in the bunker. Leave one leg outside the bunker, with the knee flexed, and the majority of the weight on the one inside. Stay centred over the ball, pick the club up sharply (especially if the lip is close behind the club) and use a wristy follow-through to scoop the ball up quickly. Above all ensure that you have enough loft to get the ball out of the bunker. Remember to make contact with the sand first, not the ball. If the ball is hard up against the front lip, requiring instant elevation, have the clubface well open at address.

Dinah keeps her right foot outside the bunker, but her weight on the foot inside

When the ball is close to the back lip of the bunker, a sharp pick-up of the club is required

Note how little body movement is required to play the shot. Dinah has stayed centred over the ball, scooping it out

With the ball close to the front lip, keep your left foot outside the bunker and open the clubface wide for instant elevation

If your ball runs into a water hazard you may feel that it is worthwhile to play it as it lies. Otherwise have no hesitation in accepting the penalty stroke rather than wasting two or three shots trying to extricate yourself, as Payne Stewart did to his cost in his Ryder Cup singles match with Jose Maria Olazabal in 1989.

A rule of thumb should be that if the ball is completely submerged beneath the water take the penalty drop. If a quarter or more of the ball is above the water-line maybe it is worth the risk.

First take off your shoes and socks. Do not touch the water with your club. The same rule applies here as in the bunker. First close the clubface. Then pick the club up sharply, hitting hard down through impact. As in the bunker hit about an inch behind the ball and aim to remove the piece of water that is directly behind the ball. Most important, do not quit on the shot. Imagine yourself in tough rough, needing a strong shot to move the ball out.

If you discover that your ball has come to rest against an immovable object that is not ruled an obstruction you are faced with two alternatives. Either you can hit it hard against the object and hope for a good ricochet, or you can choose the more skilful but safer option and play a one-handed backhand shot.

Stand with your back to your destination with the ball a few inches from the right foot. Hold the club in your favoured hand and address the ball with the clubface pointing towards the destination. Make an upright swing back from the ball with an immediate flexing of the wrist, and let the club swing down and through. Don't try and hit the ball too hard. You do not want to make an air shot.

When faced with having to play a shot from a kneeling position, you will be surprised how far you can still hit the ball. First, if the ground is wet, by all means wear waterproof trousers, but don't kneel on a golf towel which is seen as unfairly improving your stance and will incur a penalty stroke.

You will obviously have to use a very flat swing, so start by gripping the club down at the beginning of the shaft, then follow the usual guidelines for a swing – rotate the trunk and imagine yourself sweeping the ball off its lie.

Sometimes you will find your ball resting against an object which will force you to play left-handed. It would not help much to be ambidextrous unless you have left-handed clubs in your bag!

You need to use a club with a big face, so the sand wedge would be best. Don't try and make too big a backswing – waist-high is far enough so that you can still control the stroke. Keep a smooth rhythm on the downswing, eye always on the ball, and flick the ball forward off its lie.

GETTING WHAT YOU CAN OUT OF THE GAME

Well, that more or less wraps it up. There's not much more that I can teach you as regards shotmaking. There's enough in what you have read so far to make you a scratch golfer.

However, learning how to play the game is not golf's only problem. Many instruction books will teach you how to play the key golf shots, but give no advice on how to join a club, or how to get a handicap, or what courses you can play on.

With golf becoming more and more popular all over the world more and more people want to take up the game, but, in Britain particularly, there simply are not enough courses to go round. Club membership is like gold dust, but once in, and when you know what competitions are open to you and the various scoring systems used, there is no limit to the enjoyment to be gained from this game.

How to join a club

This is perhaps the hardest part of the game. There is an old saying in club golf: 'You can't join a club until you have a handicap and you can't get a handicap until you have joined a club'. It's a bit like the Equity Card Catch 22 situation, and sadly it's no great distortion of the truth.

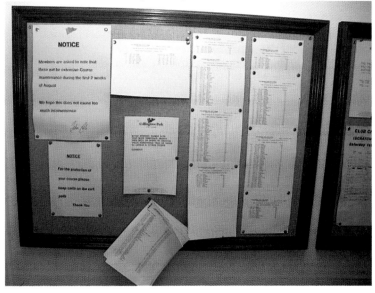

SUNDAY

The first step is to find a suitable club, one that has room for more golfers. Make sure that you like the course and that it's not too difficult. You want to enjoy your rounds of golf, not dread them like an injection.

Such is the demand that many clubs have long waiting-lists, particularly those in close proximity to big cities. If you are young enough join as a junior and stay on (provided you can afford the increase in subscription fees) until you are a senior (over 18). Alternatively take out five-day membership – weekdays only – or consider a country membership, which allows you a cut-price subscription if you live a long way from the club during the week.

You will need to be proposed and seconded by someone who is already a member. You will then be judged on your golfing skill and etiquette (the latter is more important than the former!) by the secretary or professional, and if you pass that test there should be nothing to stop you from joining the club.

However, there is more to a golf club than just the golf. It is also a great social venue, so the mix of members is important.

Finally, make sure the club is affiliated to the national golfing union which oversees handicaps. Unless the club is registered with them you cannot get a legitimate handicap.

Getting a handicap

Handicaps are important. Certainly you can play the game without one, but you will get so much more enjoyment from it if you take the time to get a handicap registered at your club.

A handicap is a guide to the standard of your game. The lower the handicap the better you are. If your handicap is, say, 10, then on an average day you are expected to go round the course 10 over par. A scratch golfer is one who, on average, returns a score of par. Better than scratch is dealt with in plus figures, but that is usually the domain of the professional. At the other end of the spectrum, 18 is the maximum for men, 24 for a woman.

A handicap allows you to play in competitions, not only at your own club, but at others as well. It allows you to play against someone who is either better or worse than you without making the match one-sided, unlike other sports, and it allows you to go on golfing holidays, both in this country and overseas. You can take a handicap certificate with you, signed by your club secretary, which proves to other clubs that you are of a satisfactory standard to play on their course.

There is no mystery about getting a handicap. Processes differ from club to club, but generally you have to play your course with a fellow member who will mark your card as you go round. Hand it in to the secretary, and when you have two or three cards the secretary can work out your average score and determine your handicap.

Hand in two or three cards to determine your handicap

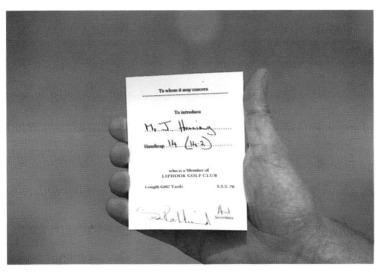

A handicap certificate is a guarantee of your golfing ability

Handicaps do not, and should not, remain constant. Each competition round you play will alter your handicap by a fraction of a stroke. There is no need to go into the finer details of how the handicap system works – it's complicated at the best of times. Leave that to the secretary and his mathematics.

There may be a temptation to keep your handicap at an inappropriately high level so that you can keep winning competitions. Nothing is more likely to incur the wrath of fellow golfers than this 'banditry'. There should be a great deal of personal pride gained from achieving as low a handicap as possible.

The different scoring systems

There are many variations on the scoring systems in golf. They all have their merits and only heighten enjoyment of the game. As I have remarked before, players of opposite standards can play with and against one another without the game being a mis-match.

Strokeplay is the system most commonly used in professional golf and it is also probably the simplest. Just tot up the number of shots played in a round and whoever has played fewer wins. Let us assume that a player with a 10 handicap plays against someone with a 16 handicap. At the end the number of shots are deducted from the total according to the handicap.

Another popular format is **matchplay**. Whoever plays the fewer shots on the first hole wins that particular hole and goes 'one up' – one up with 17 to play, assuming it's an 18-hole course. When there are too few holes left for the player in arrears to win or draw level, the match is over. The trouble with this format is that quite often the match is over before the 18th.

If the 10- and 16-handicappers are playing this system, one takes two-thirds of the difference—in this case two-thirds of six is four—and that number of shots is given to the lesser player. In other words, on the four toughest holes on the course (as marked on the card under 'Stroke' 1–4) the par for the lesser player is one more than stated.

The **Stableford** system is very popular, particularly if more than two golfers are playing in the same group. Many club events, at junior level especially, use this system as it is so simple.

Let us take our 10-handicapper as an example again. The course gives him 10 shots – one each at the 10 hardest holes (as marked on the card under 'Stroke' 1–10). On the other eight holes the par for him is as stated, so he will collect no points for a double-bogey or worse, one point for a bogey, two points for a par, three for a birdie and four for an eagle. An albatross, should he be so lucky, is worth five points.

On the holes where he has shots the par is one more than stated. So if he plays a par-4 hole in regulation figures he will have a nett birdie, worth three points. If he takes six then he has a nett five and one point, and so on.

This format is almost the best of the lot as it makes such good use of the handicap system and also ensures quick play, as one can pick up on a hole if there is no chance of scoring any points.

Playing competitions

Playing in club competitions is one very good way to improve at golf. It is then that the mental aspect of the game, which is so important, comes into play. How well you keep your game intact at this stage will determine the result and you will discover just how good a golfer you really are. You may be able to thrash your brother in a Sunday morning friendly, but are you strong enough to keep the club champion at bay in a head-to-head?

As in tennis you can also play doubles – or pairs as golfers call it – either in a fourball with your opponents or as a twoball, with you and your partner taking alternate shots. This is called **foursomes** golf, the added pressure being that you may mess up after your partner has put you in the perfect spot.

A variation on this is a **greensome**, when you and your partner both hit drives on every hole and you then play the best of the two, playing alternate shots thereafter.

Mixed foursomes is an enjoyable variation of the game . . .

. . . but it can often lead to marital arguments!

Of course you can also play mixed foursomes golf, which I know from experience has ruined many a friendly alliance!

The Americans are probably the best at coming up with exciting alternative forms of competitions, the most popular being **skins**. Two or more can play and each person puts up a sum of money per hole. The person who wins the hole wins the pot. If the hole is halved the pot is carried over to the next hole, and so on until there is an outright winner. It is not unusual for a very large sum of money to be won on one hole. The idea is much the same as that of a jackpot at a race-track.

There are many variations that you can play, though your home club will tend to stick to the orthodox systems. The others are best kept for play among friends.

Incidentally, once you belong to a club and have a handicap registered there is nothing wrong with a friend entering you as a guest in a competition at his home club, though if you win too often you may find yourself not being asked back – or else declared a 'bandit'!

Courses you can play

These days there are four categories of golf courses or clubs.

First the **private members club**, run by the members for the members, and in many cases, owned by the members as well. Anyone can play on these courses, but you may find that you have to be introduced by, and then play with, a member. Weekends are often members only, and during the week the courses are sometimes quite empty, but do remember to bring handicap cards with you just in case. Examples of private clubs are Sunningdale and Walton Heath.

Sunningdale is a beautiful example of a private members club

St Andrews, the home of golf, is a municipal course

Then there is the **municipal course** where anyone of any standard can play as long as a tee-time is booked in advance. There is no dress code, green fees are much cheaper than at any other course, but the quality is often rather poor – except for St Andrews, which many forget is a municipal course, where the quality is quite superb. Municipal golf facilities, owned by the local councils, also include driving-ranges.

Proprietary-owned courses are the ones owned by big companies on a money-making basis. Golf clubs never used to be run this way, but golf today is such big business that this corporate money is increasing. Frankly this is an alarming trend. Prices are much higher at this category of club, but you do tend to get better service in the restaurants and bars afterwards. Anyone can play on these courses, but you have to book well in advance, and the prices are prohibitive. Wentworth, in Surrey, is an example.

Wentworth, a proprietary-owned club

Finally there's the **resort course**, very similar to the proprietary-owned club, the difference being that the course is a facility attached to a hotel along with tennis courts, swimming-pool, conference rooms etc. Gleneagles, in Scotland, is a good example, where you cannot play the courses unless you are staying in the hotel.

Stay at the Gleneagles Hotel and you can play the excellent courses

GLOSSARY

air shot making a shot but missing the ball

albatross a hole played in three strokes below regulation figures

bandit a slang term for a player with an unfairly high handicap

birdie a hole played in one stroke below regulation figures

bogey a hole played in one stroke over regulation figures

borrow the slope on a green

break the movement of a ball on the green

bunker a sand-filled hazard

chip-and-run a shot played deliberately along the ground

cup the hole on the green that the ball falls into

cutspin imparted to the ball so it will stop quickly upon landing

divot a piece of turf removed from the course by a club

double-bogey a hole played in two strokes over regulation figures

draw the ball's flightpath that moves slightly right to left

drive a shot played from a tee

driver a club used to hit long shots, usually from a tee

eagle a hole played in two strokes below regulation figures

etiquette golf's code of behaviour

fade the ball's flightpath that moves slightly left to right

fairway the mown strip of grass between tee and green

flag the hole (a flag is usually on the top of the *pin*)

foursomes when partners take alternate shots

green the putting surface

greensome when partners take separate tee shots, choose the best of them and play alternate shots from there

grip the padded part at the top of the club; the position your hands take on the club

handicap a guide to the standard of your golf

hook a shot that moves sharply right to left in the air

iron an iron club

lie the position in which your ball rests after a shot

long game the long shots with the woods and long irons, etc.

matchplay a scoring system based on number of holes won

medal a club competition

out-of-bounds a designated area where a player incurs penalty shots if the ball lands there

GLOSSARY

par   regulation number of strokes for a hole or a course
pin   the hole
pitch   a short shot with loft
putt   a shot on the green, usually played with a putter
putter   a club used to take putts

rough   a hazard consisting of uncut grass

sand wedge   a club with maximum clubface loft, usually for bunker shots
scratch   a standard of play that is in line with the par of the course
set-up   the fundamental body position adopted before taking a shot
shaft   the part of the club from the clubface to the grip
shank   a destructive shot that flies almost at right angles
short game   the short shots with wedges, etc.
skins   a scoring system with money on each hole
slice   a shot that moves sharply left to right in the air
Stableford   a scoring system with points on each hole according to one's handicap
strokeplay   a scoring system based on number of strokes played

takeaway   the first few feet of the backswing
tee   the flat area from where the first shot on any hole is played
tee peg   on which the ball can be placed on a tee
twoball (three-, four-)   the number of balls played in one group

wedge   a club with a lofted clubface for short shots
wood   a wooden club